001

LONDON GWR

002

003

004

006

005

007

BRIDLINGTON

008

NORTH BERWICK

009

010

011

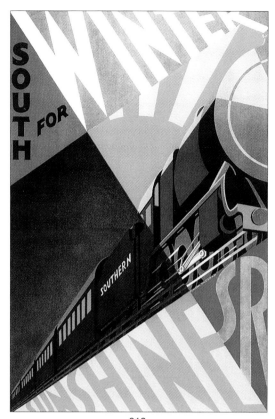

012

013

014

015

016

017

018

019

020

021

022

023

024

025

026

027

028

029

030

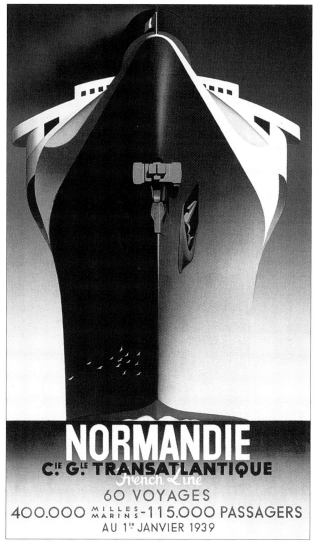

031

032

033

034

035

036

037

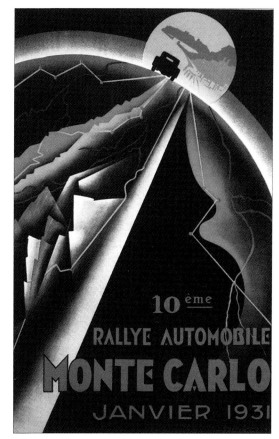

038

039

040

041

ROME

Par le train de luxe "ROME EXPRESS"

043

044

042

045

DOLOMITES
LES MONTAGNES AUX REFLETS DE FLAMMES
60 VILLÉGIATURES - 30.000 LITS

046

049

047

048

050

051

052

053

054

055

056

057

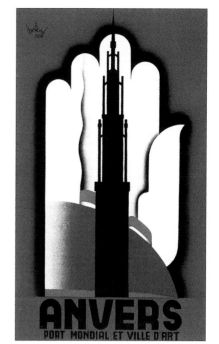

058

059

060

061

062

064

065

063

066

067

068

069

070

071

072

075

073

076

074

077

078

079

080

081

082

083

084

085

086

087

088

089

090

091

092

093

094

095

096

100

097

098

101

099

102

MARLBOROUGH SOUNDS
GOV'T TOURIST DEP'T **NEW ZEALAND**

103

Famous LAKES, MOUNTAINS, FIORDS.
Otago & Southland

South Island
NEW ZEALAND

104

Mt. Egmont. 8,260 ft.
NEW ZEALAND

105

GOV'T TOURIST DEP'T **MT COOK**
NEW ZEALAND

106

FOR THE WORLDS BEST SPORT
GOV'T TOURIST DEP'T **NEW ZEALAND**

107

108

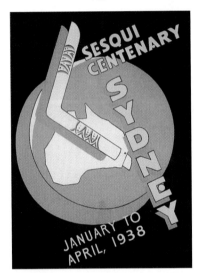

109

111

110

112

113

114

115

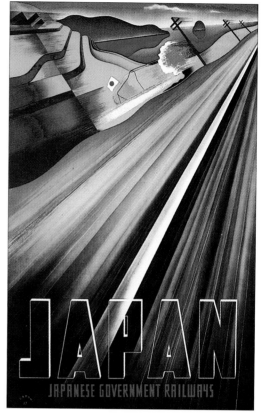

116

117

118

119

120

121

122

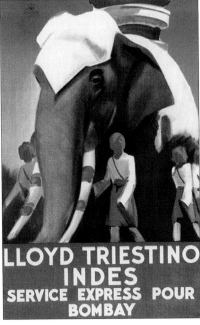

123

124

125

126

127

128

129

130

131

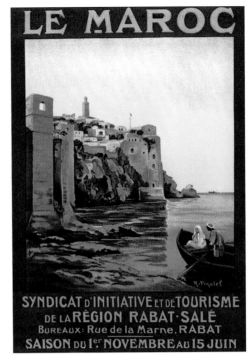

134

132

133

135

136

137

138

139

140

143

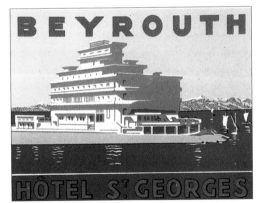

141

142

144

26 *Palestine, Lebanon, Egypt and Algeria*

145

146

147

148

149

150

153

151

154

152

155

156

157

158

159

160

161

162

163

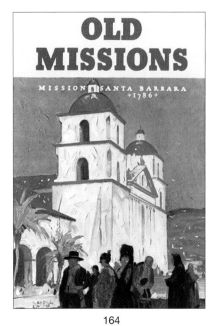

164

165

166

167

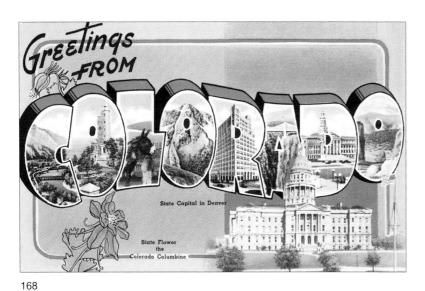

168

171

169

172

170

173

174

175

176

177

178

179

180

181

182

183

184

185

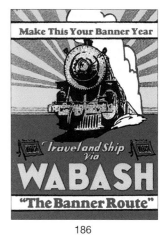

186

187

188

189

190

191

192

193

196

197

194

195

198

199

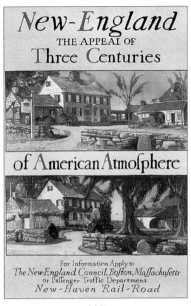

200

201

202

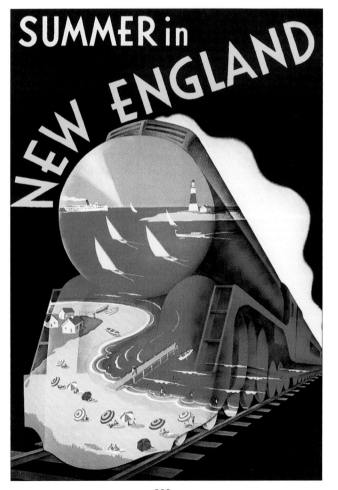

203

204

207

208

205

209

206

210

211

212

214

213

215

216

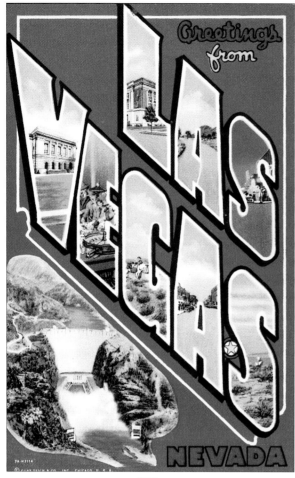

217

219

220

218

221

222

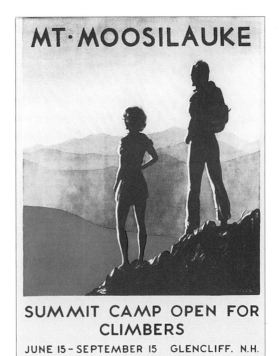

225

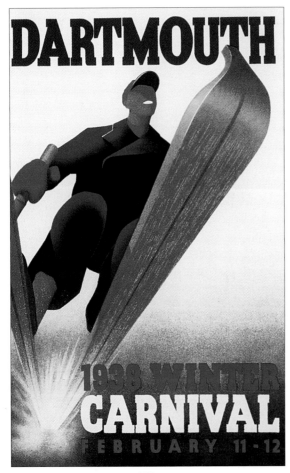

223

224

226

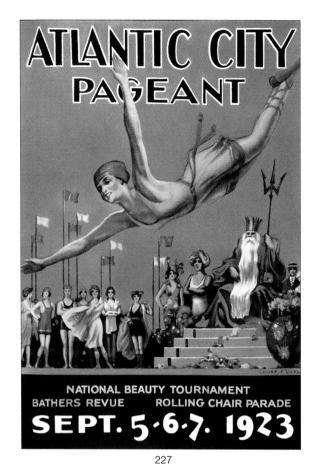

227

228

229

230

231

232

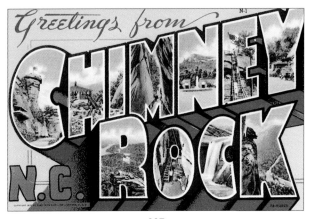

235

233

236

234

237

238

242

239

240

241

243

244

245

248

246

249

250

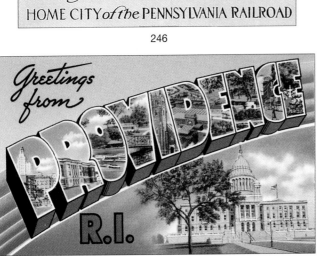

247

251

252

256

253

257

254

258

255

259

260

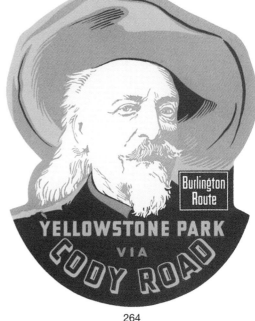

264

261

265

262

266

263

46 United States

267

270

268

271

269

272

273

274

276

275

277

278

48 *Bermuda, Brazil, Antilles, Jamaica and Panama*

■SCHOLASTIC

READ & RES

Bringing the best books to life in the classroom

Activities based on

Wonder

By R.J. Palacio

FOR AGES 7–11

Scholastic Education, an imprint of Scholastic Ltd
Book End, Range Road, Witney, Oxfordshire, OX29 0YD
Registered office: Westfield Road, Southam, Warwickshire CV47 0RA

Printed and bound by Ashford Colour Press
© 2018 Scholastic Ltd
3 4 5 6 7 8 9   8 9 0 1 2 3 4 5 6 7

British Library Cataloguing-in-Publication Data
A catalogue record for this book is available from the British Library.
ISBN 978-1407-18252-0

Extracts from *The National Curriculum in England, English Programme of Study* © Crown Copyright. Reproduced under the terms of the Open Government Licence (OGL). http://www.nationalarchives.gov.uk/doc/open-government-licence/version/3

Due to the nature of the web, we cannot guarantee the content or links of any site mentioned. We strongly recommend that teachers check websites before using them in the classroom.

Authors Eileen Jones
Editorial team Rachel Morgan, Vicki Yates, Sarah Snashall, Suzanne Adams
Series designers Neil Salt and Alice Duggan
Designer Alice Duggan
Illustrator Camille Medina/Beehive Illustration

Acknowledgements
The publishers gratefully acknowledge permission to reproduce the following material:
The Random House Group for the use of the text extracts and cover from *Wonder* by RJ Palacio.
Text © 2012. (Bodley Head)

Every effort has been made to trace copyright holders for the works reproduced in this book, and the publishers apologise for any inadvertent omissions.

CONTENTS ▽

How to use Read & Respond in your classroom...

Read & Respond provides teaching ideas related to a specific well-loved children's book. Each Read & Respond book is divided into the following sections:

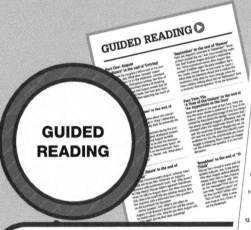

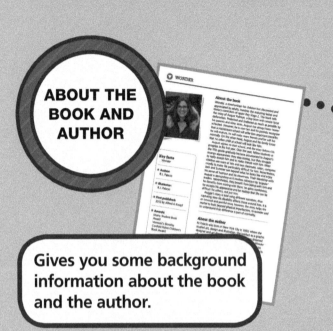

ABOUT THE BOOK AND AUTHOR

Gives you some background information about the book and the author.

GUIDED READING

Breaks the book down into sections and gives notes for using it with guided reading groups. A bookmark has been provided on page 12 containing comprehension questions. The children can be directed to refer to these as they read.

SHARED READING

Provides extracts from the children's book with associated notes for focused work. There is also one non-fiction extract that relates to the children's book.

GRAMMAR, PUNCTUATION & SPELLING

Provides word-level work related to the children's book so you can teach grammar, punctuation and spelling in context.

PLOT, CHARACTER & SETTING

Contains activity ideas focused on the plot, characters and the setting of the story.

GET WRITING

Provides writing activities related to the children's book. These activities may be based directly on the children's book or be broadly based on the themes and concepts of the story.

TALK ABOUT IT

Has speaking and listening activities related to the children's book. These activities may be based directly on the children's book or be broadly based on the themes and concepts of the story.

ASSESSMENT

Contains short activities that will help you assess whether the children have understood concepts and curriculum objectives. They are designed to be informal activities to feed into your planning.

" The titles are great fun to use and cover exactly the range of books that children most want to read. It makes it easy to explore texts fully and ensure the children want to keep on reading more. **"**

Chris Flanagan, Year 5 Teacher,
St Thomas of Canterbury
Primary School

Activities

The activities follow the same format:

- **Objective:** the objective for the lesson. It will be based upon a curriculum objective, but will often be more specific to the focus being covered.

- **What you need:** a list of resources you need to teach the lesson, including photocopiable pages.

- **What to do:** the activity notes.

- **Differentiation:** this is provided where specific and useful differentiation advice can be given to support and/or extend the learning in the activity. Differentiation by providing additional adult support has not been included as this will be at a teacher's discretion based upon specific children's needs and ability, as well as the availability of support.

The activities are numbered for reference within each section and should move through the text sequentially – so you can use the lesson while you are reading the book. Once you have read the book, most of the activities can be used in any order you wish.

Section	Activity	Curriculum objectives
Guided reading		Comprehension: To draw inferences such as inferring characters' feelings, thoughts and motives from their actions, and justifying inferences with evidence.
Shared reading	1	Comprehension: To predict what might happen from details stated and implied.
	2	Comprehension: To draw inferences such as inferring characters' feelings, thoughts and motives from their actions, and justifying inferences with evidence.
	3	Comprehension: To check that the book makes sense to them, discussing their understanding and exploring the meaning of words in context.
	4	Comprehension: To distinguish between statements of fact and opinion.
Grammar, punctuation & spelling	1	Comprehension: To discuss and evaluate how authors use language, considering the impact on the reader.
	2	Vocabulary, grammar and punctuation: To use commas to clarify meaning or to avoid ambiguity in writing.
	3	Vocabulary, grammar and punctuation: To use passive verbs to affect the presentation of information in a sentence.
	4	Vocabulary, grammar and punctuation: To use relative clauses beginning with 'who', 'which', 'where', 'when', 'whose', 'that' or with an implied... relative pronoun.
	5	Vocabulary, grammar and punctuation: To recognise vocabulary and structures that are appropriate for formal speech and writing.
	6	Vocabulary, grammar and punctuation: To recognise that words are related by meaning as synonyms and antonyms.
Plot, character & setting	1	Comprehension: To ask questions to improve their understanding of the text.
	2	Comprehension: To draw inferences such as inferring characters' feelings, thoughts and motives from their actions, and justify inferences with evidence.
	3	Comprehension: To check that the book makes sense to them, discussing their understanding and exploring the meaning of words in context.
	4	Comprehension: To draw inferences such as inferring characters' feelings, thoughts and motives from their actions, and justify inferences with evidence.
	5	Comprehension: To discuss and evaluate how authors use language... considering the impact on the reader.
	6	Comprehension: To read books that are structured in different ways...
	7	Comprehension: To identify and discuss themes and conventions in and across a wide range of writing.
	8	Comprehension: To identify and discuss themes and conventions in and across a wide range of writing.

Section	Activity	Curriculum objectives
Talk about it	**1**	Spoken language: To participate in discussions... and debates.
	2	Spoken language: To use spoken language to develop understanding through speculating, hypothesising, imagining and exploring ideas.
	3	Spoken language: To give well-structured... narratives for different purposes, including for expressing feelings.
	4	Spoken language: To participate... in role play... Comprehension: To infer characters' feelings, thoughts and motives.
	5	Spoken language: To consider and evaluate different viewpoints, attending to and building on the contributions of others.
	6	Spoken language: To use spoken language to develop understanding through speculating, hypothesising, imagining and exploring ideas.
Get writing	**1**	Composition: To draft and write by précising longer passages.
	2	Composition: To select the appropriate form and use other similar writing as models for their own.
	3	Composition: To note and develop initial ideas...
	4	Composition: To identify the audience for and purpose of their writing, selecting the appropriate form and using other similar writing as models for their own.
	5	Composition: To select appropriate grammar and vocabulary, understanding how such choices can change and enhance meaning.
	6	Composition: To describe settings, characters and atmosphere and integrate dialogue.
Assessment	**1**	Comprehension: To predict what might happen from details stated and implied.
	2	Vocabulary, grammar and punctuation: To use and understand the grammar and grammatical terminology in English Appendix 2.
	3	Comprehension: To identify and discuss themes and conventions across a wide range of writing.
	4	Composition: To select appropriate grammar and vocabulary, understanding how such choices can change and enhance meaning.
	5	Composition: To identify the audience for and purpose of their writing, selecting the appropriate form and using other similar writing as models for their own.
	6	Composition: To identify the audience for and purpose of their writing, selecting the appropriate form and using other similar writing as models for their own.

Key facts
Wonder

◉ **Author:**
RJ Palacio

◉ **Illustrator:**
RJ Palacio

◉ **First published:**
2012 by Alfred A Knopf

◉ **Awards:**
Maine Student Book
Award
Vermont's Dorothy
Canfield Fisher Children's
Book Award

◉ **Did you know?**
Wonder has been
translated into many
languages and has been
adapted for a film version,
released in 2017.

About the book

Wonder, a novel written for children but discovered and appreciated by adults, matches the maturing tastes and literacy curriculum of upper Key Stage 2. The book tells the story of August Pullman, a boy born with severe facial deformities. Protected and sheltered as much as possible by his parents and older sister, August has always been home-schooled. However, he is now ten and his parents recognise that a mainstream school will offer him important benefits: he will mature, he will make more friends and he will live normally. On the other hand, August and his family know that no other child at school will look like him.

August agrees to start school, and the story follows his progress in his first year. Over the year, fellow students in the fifth grade gradually become accustomed to August's strange appearance; they stop staring, but they struggle to really accept him and to make friends with him. Most children are wary of him and one classmate, Julian, conspires cruelly to make life particularly difficult for him. Nevertheless, Jack and Summer see beyond what he looks like and enjoy his sense of humour and his cleverness. Their friendship with August is demanding as it involves ostracism by 'popular' leaders. Nevertheless, they benefit from being with him and he benefits from mixing with them: he gains confidence, he accepts his appearance and he realises that life can be difficult for others, not just him.

Auggie's story is told using different narrators, thus capturing how his disability affects those around him. It is an unusual and painful issue, however, the story helps the reader to look beyond physical imperfection, to wonder and to understand that difference is part of normality.

About the author

RJ Palacio was born in New York City in 1963, where she studied art, design and illustration. She worked as a graphic designer and art director for 20 years, but always dreamed of writing and illustrating her own book. She wrote *Wonder* after an incident with her son. While they were waiting to buy an ice cream, her son saw a girl with facial birth defects. Palacio feared that he would react badly and embarrass the girl and her family, so she hurried her son away. In doing this, Palacio later felt that she had made the situation worse. Her book is an attempt to prepare other children and parents for seeing and accepting someone who looks different.

Palacio's real name is Raquel Jamillo. She took the pen name RJ Palacio in order to follow the Latin tradition of using her Colombian mother's name as her pen name.

GUIDED READING ▶

Part One: August
'Ordinary' to the end of 'Driving'

Read aloud the song lyrics before and at the start of Part One. Ask: *What does 'wonder' mean?* Discuss question 12 on the bookmark. Comment on the confiding, first-person writing; fast flow of information; matter-of-fact delivery of shocking statements. Point out that August reveals that he is starting school next week, but then goes back into the past. Ask: *Is Mom expecting too much of August?*

'Paging Mr Tushman' to the end of 'Home'

Ask: *What does August notice about Mrs Garcia?* (Her eyes drop and her smile is 'shiny'.) *What does 'shiny' suggest?* (forced) *Why does he eventually like her?* (She reassures Mom.)

Identify Julian's unpleasantness during the tour: lack of eye contact; avoidance of physical contact; tactless questioning; making August stumble backwards. Get children to re-read the dialogue in the second part of 'The Performance Space', for discussion of question 5 on the bookmark. Point out the final sentence in 'Home'. Ask: *What does it reveal about August?*

'First-Day Jitters' to the end of 'Padawan'

Identify that Charlotte greets August, whereas Julian pretends not to see him. Comment on August's experience with combination locks. Ask: *Why doesn't he help Henry?* Discuss Julian's apparent friendliness when he talks to August about *Star Wars* characters. Ask: *How is he cruel?* (He aks whether August likes the character with a deformed face.) Use question 4 on the bookmark for discussion.

Define 'precept'. Ask: *What is the effect on August of Mr Browne's lesson?* (He will like school, no matter what.) Ask: *Why do you think August cuts off his plait? Are his final tears surprising?*

'September' to the end of 'Names'

Point out August's comment in 'September': 'None of them looked like me.' Ask: *How would this make him feel?* Explore August and Jack's relationship. Ask: *What unpleasant events does August later accept?* (Children reject his party invitation; he is the 'moldy cheese' that no one wants to touch.) *What does his tolerance show?* (He is used to this treatment.) *Why does he react strongly when he hears children talking about him on Halloween?* (Jack is involved.) Discuss question 10 on the bookmark.

Part Two: Via
'A Tour of the Galaxy' to the end of 'An Apparition at the Door'

Read the quote at the start of Part Two. Point out that this space theme is continued in 'A Tour of the Galaxy' with the powerful image of the Sun (August) orbited by the planets (his family). Comment that Via has always accepted August's difference. Ask: *What changed when she stayed with Grans? Why did she wish she could stay forever?* (People did not stare; she was the centre of attention.) Identify current problems for Via: Ella and Miranda are changing; Auggie is changing; Mom checks on Auggie, not her. Let the children use question 3 on the bookmark for discussion.

'Breakfast' to the end of 'Time to Think'

Discuss Via's refusal to travel with Miranda and her spiteful outburst. Ask: *Is she being fair on Mom? Why does August defend Miranda?* (Miranda has always been kind to him.) Point out that Miranda still asks after August. Ask: *Why does Via not pass on her messages?* Find Via's comment about Mom's two roles: 'August's mom' and 'Via's mom'. *How do they conflict? Which wins?* Discuss the events of 'Trick or Treat'. *What is revealed about Via?* (She also puts August first.) Direct the children to question 4 on the bookmark.

Part Three: Summer

Ask: *Why did Summer sit with August on the first day?* (She felt sorry for him.) *Why has she continued to sit there?* (He is fun.) Comment on Summer's ability to think for herself. Ask: *Why does she become angry with Auggie?* Examine how their relationship develops: shared confidences and jokes; taking Auggie home; working together. Let the children discuss question 1 on the bookmark. Ask: *Is Summer right to tell Jack that August overheard him at Halloween?*

Part Four: Jack
'The Call' to the end of 'Partners'

Investigate Jack's first encounter with August. Ask: *Is his 'Uhh!' excusable? Why does Veronica rush the brothers away?* Remind the children about the author's own experience. Ask: *What makes Jack agree to Mr Tushman's request?* (the meanness of his own brother) Explore the relationship between Jack and August as you discuss question 4 on the bookmark. Point out Jack's recognition that befriending August was brave. *Ask: Why was he mean about August at Halloween? How does he react now to August being called names?* Ask the children to discuss question 7 on the bookmark.

'Detention' to the end of 'Letters, Emails, Facebook, Texts'

Point out Mr Tushman's 'serious', 'expelled' and 'suspended', but his recognition that 'even nice kids do dumb things'. Ask: *How does he show concern for Jack?* (He does not want the incident on Jack's permanent record and his letter is sympathetic.) Ask: *What do you think about Mrs Albans' email? What is the tone of Mr Tushman's reply?* (He dismisses her argument about August and rejects her ignorant labels.) *What is revealed in the final text message?* (Jack and August are friends again.)

Discuss with the children the opening quotations of parts three and four. Ask: *What is emphasised – physical looks or inner feelings?* Direct the children to question 8 on the bookmark.

'Back from Winter Break' to the end of 'The Boyfriend'

Indicate when Jack is 'dissed' by other children and 'ditched' at lunch. Ask: *Why does this happen?* Comment that he grumbles that people pretend he does not exist. *What is August's sarcastic reply?* Investigate how impressed Jack is by August's house, his envy of August's room and his concern about how August's family would react to him. *Do you think that August knows that he is fortunate in many ways? Does he sometimes feel too sorry for himself?* Direct the children to question 2 on the bookmark for discussion.

Part Five: Justin

Ask: *What is different about the appearance of the text?* (Capital letters are absent.) *Is the writer presenting Justin as unusual?* Point out his initial shock at August's appearance. Contrast his casual attitude when he looks at Miranda 'blankly' when she asks if he is 'okay with it'? Ask: *Why do Justin and Via argue?* (Via has not mentioned Miranda.) Point out Justin's recognition that Via and others have to be brave because of their relationship with August. Together, discuss question 4 on the bookmark.

Part Six: August
'North Pole' to the end of 'Goodbye'

Ask: *Why does Julian lose support?* (He tells laughable lies.) Comment on August's increasing maturity as he copes with his new hearing aids casually. Emphasise important points in 'My Cave' and 'Goodbye': August's anger about the play; his expectation that Mom will follow him; Via's outburst that 'Not everything in the world is about you, Auggie'. *Ask: Is Via right to say this? Is August self-centred? If so, why?* Remind the children of Via's description of the family in 'A tour of the Galaxy' in Part Two. Discuss questions 2 and 9 on the bookmark.

'Daisy's Toys' to the end of 'The Ending'

Discuss the unifying effect Daisy's death has on the family. Point out that Mom comforts Via, not August; he puts himself to bed. Ask: *What further sign is there that August is growing up?* (He does not want Dad to call him 'Auggie Doggie'.) Point out that Justin thoughtfully diverts Mr Davenport when he 'froze' on meeting August. Ask: *Why does August panic? Who rescues him?* Let the children discuss question 10 on the bookmark.

Part Seven: Miranda

Remind the children that the reader is now viewing events previously described from Via's point of view. Ask: *How is Miranda's summer difficult? Why does she lie about having a deformed brother?* Examine how her relationship with Via goes wrong: lack of contact; feeling awkward; becoming different. Identify proof that Miranda still cares about Via and her family: persuading Mr Davenport not to use a hurtful play; applying for a role while expecting Via to get it; ringing their house 'hoping Via would answer'; refusing to go on stage; joining the family for dinner; feeling 'absolutely happy'.

Together discuss question 6 on the bookmark.

Part Eight: August
'The Fifth-Grade Nature Retreat' to the end of 'The Woods Are Alive'

Remind the children that the nature trip is August's first night away from his parents. How does he feel about it? (nervous and excited) Indicate Mom's comment about August growing up. Ask: *What are signs of his increasing maturity?* (He decides not to take his *Star Wars* bag; he leaves Baboo at home; he takes down his poster; he puts himself to bed.)

'Alien' to the end of 'Sleep'

Point out how August tries to stop the attackers by reasoning that he and Jack are small. Identify the cruel insults: 'alien', 'freak' and 'orc'. Comment on Jack's desire to protect August and the courage of Amos. Ask: *Is it surprising that Henry pulls him to safety? Why does August cry so much afterwards? How do the others react to his tears?* (They are kind and supportive.) Comment that August is aware that 'Something had changed'. Are the other fifth-graders now on his side? Ask: *What stops August falling asleep?* (He remembers the horror on the girl's face and Eddie's hatred.)

'Aftermath' to the end of 'Ducks'

Identify friendliness to August as the children leave the bus and Mr Tushman's 'quick, tight hug'. Ask: *Is it surprising that August talks so positively to his parents about the trip? What is 'the shift' that August discovers?* (He is now 'little dude', accepted and liked; only Julian continues to ignore him.) Discuss question 9 on the bookmark.

'The Last Precept' to the end of 'Appendix'

Look together at the quotation at the beginning of part eight. Encourage the children to explain it. Ask: *What does August's shorter hair suggest? Is he more confident about being seen?* Ask: *What is Mr Tushman's main message to the students?* (Be kinder than is necessary.) *Why is August awarded his prize?* (His inner strength has captured most hearts.) Together discuss question 11 on the bookmark. Comment on the happy ending and title word in the final sentence of 'The Walk Home'. Together discuss question 12 on the bookmark. Ask: *Do the children's precepts suit their characters? Does August recognise why he won his medal and a standing ovation?* Discuss the themes that emerge from the story: tolerance and kindness to one another; accepting differences; friendship; recognising the difficulties of others.

Wonder
by R.J. Palacio

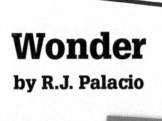

Focus on...
Meaning

1. What has made August different from everyone else? How does he feel about being different?

2. What do you think RJ Palacio wants the reader to feel about August? Does she want her character to be pitied or respected? Explain your answer.

3. What predictions can you make about what may happen in this part from its opening quotation?

4. Why is August's face always important in this story? How does it affect the behaviour and feelings of other characters? What message is the author giving to the reader?

Focus on...
Organisation

5. Do you think the author uses dialogue effectively? Give an example and explain how it adds to the story.

6. Why has the author divided the story into short subsections? Do you find this a helpful device?

Wonder
by R.J. Palacio

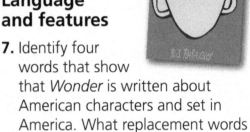

Focus on...
Language and features

7. Identify four words that show that *Wonder* is written about American characters and set in America. What replacement words would you use?

8. Why do you think Palacio opens each part with a quotation? What messages do they contain? Is this an effective feature?

Focus on...
Purpose, viewpoints and effects

9. How do other characters change their attitude to August? Why? What changes can you identify in August?

10. Is the author making an important point here or is she just making the story dramatic?

11. What is the effect of the standing ovation when August receives his award? Do you think that it brings the story to a climax? How?

12. What is the author's aim in this part of the book? How does the author achieve this?

SHARED READING ▶

Extract 1

- In this extract from Part One, August, after enduring rude questions from Julian about his face, finds himself smiling at Jack.

- Circle 'I' in the first two sentences. Ask: *What is this style of writing called?* (first-person narrative) *How is it special?* (The story is written from one person's point of view.) Circle 'I' and 'me' and identify them as personal pronouns. Locate other personal pronouns in the extract. Underline 'my' and identify it as a possessive adjective that describes 'face'.

- Ask: *Why are there so many speech marks?* (The text is mainly dialogue.) Together, work out who is speaking when no speech tag is provided. Ask: *What can we predict about the characters from what they say?* (Jack is kind, a peacemaker; Julian is unkind; Charlotte likes to be right.)

- Ask: *Was August right to correct Julian's English?* Comment on August's courage in looking at Julian and correcting his earlier mistake with 'supposedly'. Ask: *What can the reader infer about August?* (He is confident intellectually.)

- Underline the penultimate paragraph. Ask: *Is Julian's apology sincere? What implies that his action was deliberate?* (Julian has been unpleasant throughout the tour.)

- Ask: *Can you make predictions about these children's future school relationships with August? How might August's relationship with Julian develop? Which child is August most likely to be friends with?* (Point out that Jack recognises that August is smiling.) *Ask: What other predictions can we make?* (Perhaps that August will stand up for himself, that he will do well academically.)

Extract 2

- In this extract near the end of part One, August, unrecognised in his Halloween costume, listens to a classroom conversation about himself.

- Read the first sentence aloud. Circle 'him'. Ask: *Why does it seem offensive?* (The speakers are not bothering to name August.) Identify and circle other insults in these early lines: 'shrunken heads', 'orc', 'Darth Sidious'. Ask: *Why has Julian chosen the costume he wears?* (Like August, the character's face is disfigured.)

- Investigate how the identity of the second mummy is revealed gradually. Number these clues: he hangs out with August; teachers seat them next each other in class. Underline 'I knew the shrug, of course. I knew the voice.' Ask: *Why are these words important?* (August knows the mummy's identity; and it is a close friend.)

- Circle 'I knew' beginning three consecutive sentences. Ask: *What is the effect of the repetition?* Suggest that the writer builds the emotional atmosphere and the intensity of August's feelings. Ask: *Why does August stay in the classroom?*

- Ask: *What can we infer about Jack here?* (Perhaps that he is not brave enough to stand up for his friend, he cannot come to terms with August's face.) Ask: *Are you surprised that Jack says these things? Do you think he will follow Julian's advice?* Encourage discussion.

Extract 3

- In this extract, from Part Eight, August returns to school after the nature retreat to find that attitudes to him, and to Julian, have changed. Circle 'shift' in the first paragraph and comment on its frequency. Ask the children to define the word to a partner before you share meanings. Agree on 'change'.

- Read the first four sentences of paragraph one aloud. Highlight the 'size' adjectives used about the change: 'big', 'monumental,' 'seismic', 'cosmic'. Point out their increase in extent. Ask: *Why does the writer do this?* (She is emphasising the size of this change as August attempts to capture it.)

- Direct the children to the rest of paragraph one. *Ask: What happens to the story of the incident at the retreat?* Point out how it also grows, almost like a traditional tale told and retold round the fire. Identify and underline exaggerated details: 'major fistfight'; 'whole long adventure'; 'cornfield maze'; 'deep dark woods'.

- Underline the sentence 'I got picked on' to 'protected me.' Ask: *Why is this sentence important?* (It contains the essential facts of what happened at the retreat.)

- Read aloud the sentence beginning, 'And now that they'd protected me...'. Circle the word 'different'. Ask: *Why is there a different attitude to August now? How has protecting August changed people's feelings about him?* Underline 'little dude' and 'knuckle-punch'. Ask: *Why are both friendly gestures important to August?* (Other children are talking to and touching him.)

- Direct the children to paragraph two. Ask: *What other major shift has occurred? Is Julian's power affected?* (He is alone now in his ill-treatment of August and Jack.)

Extract 4

- Ask: *What is the purpose of this extract?* Underline the opening statement. Ask: *What does it achieve?* (It introduces the subject.) Read aloud the next sentence and discuss the first paragraph's function. Ask: *What questions are answered?* ('Who?', 'Why?', 'How?' and 'When?') Move on to circle the subheadings, discussing their purpose (to divide the text into distinct sections and to help the reader find information).

- Circle dates, places and names in the extract. Emphasise that they identify times and names of real people and places. Make the link between non-fiction and facts.

- Ask: *How is John Merrick linked to the novel 'Wonder'?* (facial disfigurement) Highlight 'The Elephant Man' in paragraph four. Remind the children that in *Wonder* Part Seven, Miranda persuades Mr Davenport not to put on *The Elephant Man*, a play about John Merrick.

- Underline 'was robbed' and 'was contacted'. Identify them as passive verbs. Circle and identify 'Merrick' and 'Treves' as the subjects of these passive verbs.

- Point out Merrick's wish to be 'like other people' in paragraph five. Link to August's similar thoughts in Part One of *Wonder*: 'None of them looked like me'. Discuss the difference between August's fictional and Merrick's actual experience.

- Ask: *How does the story of John Merrick make you feel?* Ask the children, in pairs, to write two sentences about how they feel about the way Merrick was treated by the people he met. Discuss these opinions and compare them with the facts in the extract. Ask: *What text type might combine both opinions and facts?* (perhaps a newspaper report)

Extract 1

Then I actually smiled. I don't know. Sometimes when I have the feeling like I'm almost crying, it can turn into an almost-laughing feeling. And that must have been the feeling I was having then, because I smiled, almost like I was going to giggle. The thing is, because of the way my face is, people who don't know me very well don't always get that I'm smiling. My mouth doesn't go up at the corners the way other people's mouths do. It just goes straight across my face. But somehow Jack Will got that I had smiled at him. And he smiled back.

"Julian's a jerk," he whispered before Julian and Charlotte reached us. "But, dude, you're gonna have to talk." He said this seriously, like he was trying to help me. I nodded as Julian and Charlotte caught up to us. We were all quiet for a second, all of us just kind of nodding, looking at the floor. Then I looked up at Julian.

"The word's 'supposedly,' by the way," I said.

"What are you talking about?"

"You said 'supposably' before," I said.

"I did not!"

"Yeah you did," Charlotte nodded. "You said the science elective is *supposably* really hard. I heard you."

"I absolutely did not," he insisted.

"Whatever," said Jack. "Let's just go."

"Yeah, let's just go," agreed Charlotte, following Jack down the stairs to the next floor. I started to follow her, but Julian cut right in front of me, which actually made me stumble backward.

"Oops, sorry about that!" said Julian.

But I could tell from the way he looked at me that he wasn't really sorry at all.

Extract 2

One of the mummies was saying: "It really does look like him."

"Like this part especially...," answered Julian's voice. He put his fingers on the cheeks and eyes of his Darth Sidious mask.

"Actually," said the mummy, "what he really looks like is one of those shrunken heads. Have you ever seen those? He looks exactly like that."

"I think he looks like an orc."

"Oh yeah!"

"If I looked like that," said the Julian voice, kind of laughing, "I swear to God, I'd put a hood over my face every day."

"I've thought about this a lot," said the second mummy, sounding serious, "and I really think ... if I looked like him, seriously, I think that I'd kill myself."

"You would not," answered Darth Sidious.

"Yeah, for real," insisted the same mummy. "I can't imagine looking in the mirror every day and seeing myself like that. It would be too awful. And getting stared at all the time."

"Then why do you hang out with him so much?" asked Darth Sidious.

"I don't know," answered the mummy. "Tushman asked me to hang out with him at the beginning of the year, and he must have told all the teachers to put us next to each other in all our classes, or something." The mummy shrugged. I knew the shrug, of course. I knew the voice. I knew I wanted to run out of the class right then and there. But I stood where I was and listened to Jack Will finish what he was saying. "I mean, the thing is: he always follows me around. What am I supposed to do?"

"Just ditch him," said Julian.

Extract 3

When I went back to school the next day, the first thing I noticed was that there was a big shift in the way things were. A monumental shift. A seismic shift. Maybe even a cosmic shift. Whatever you want to call it, it was a big shift. Everyone—not just in our grade but in every grade—had heard about what had happened to us with the seventh graders, so suddenly I wasn't known for what I'd always been known for, but for this other thing that had happened. And the story of what happened had gotten bigger and bigger each time it was told. Two days later, the way the story went was that Amos had gotten into a major fistfight with the kid, and Miles and Henry and Jack had thrown some punches at the other guys, too. And the escape across the field became this whole long adventure through a cornfield maze and into the deep dark woods. Jack's version of the story was probably the best because he's so funny, but in whatever version of the story, and no matter who was telling it, two things always stayed the same: I got picked on because of my face and Jack defended me, and those guys—Amos, Henry, and Miles— protected me. And now that they'd protected me, I was different to them. It was like I was one of them. They all called me "little dude" now—even the jocks. These big dudes I barely even knew before would knuckle-punch me in the hallways now.

Another thing to come out of it was that Amos became super popular and Julian, because he missed the whole thing, was really out of the loop. Miles and Henry were hanging out with Amos all the time now, like they switched best friends. I'd like to be able to say that Julian started treating me better, too, but that wouldn't be true. He still gave me dirty looks across the room. He still never talked to me or Jack. But he was the only one who was like that now. And me and Jack, we couldn't care less.

Extract 4

JOHN MERRICK

John Merrick was an English man with severe face and body deformities He was born in 1862 and was originally named Joseph Carey Merrick.

Early years

Merrick was born in Leicester and his unusual physical development began when he was a few years old. His forehead developed a bony lump; his lips, one arm and both feet enlarged; his skin became thick and lumpy. In addition, a fall resulted in hip damage and a permanent limp.

Childhood

Merrick's mother died when he was nine and his father soon remarried. Merrick left school when he was thirteen, but was unable to find much work. Rejected by his father and stepmother, Merrick left home. In 1879, he entered the Leicester Union Workhouse.

Adulthood

After four years in the workhouse, Merrick was employed by a group of showmen as a travelling exhibit, under the name 'The Elephant Man'. One viewer was a surgeon, named Frederick Treves, who gave Merrick his card. Sent to tour Europe, Merrick was robbed of his savings and abandoned by his road manager. He returned to England, penniless and homeless. Facial deformities made his speech unintelligible, but he still had Treves's card in his possession. Treves was contacted and Merrick was admitted to The London Hospital.

The London Hospital

Treves visited daily and learned to understand Merrick's speech. They had long conversations; Merrick expressed his desire to be 'like other people'. Merrick filled his days with reading, making cardboard models, and, after dark, walking in the adjacent courtyard.

His health gradually deteriorated during his four years at The London Hospital. He needed more nursing, had less energy and spent more time in bed. His facial deformities grew and his head became larger. He died in 1890 aged 27.

GRAMMAR, PUNCTUATION & SPELLING ▶

1. Stronger or weaker

Objective
To discuss and evaluate how writers use language.

What you need
Copies of *Wonder*.

What to do

- Complete this activity after reading 'Padawan' in Part One. Revise adverbs together. Agree that an adverb adds to the meaning of a verb and gives interest and detail.

- Explain that some adverbs modify (weaken) or intensify (strengthen) the meaning of the verb. Direct the children to 'First-Day Jitters' and the words 'I really liked Jack'. Ask: *Which word is the adverb?* ('totally') *Which word's meaning is affected?* (the verb 'liked') *What effect does it have?* (It strengthens 'liked'.) Look at 'which would have totally embarrassed me' in 'First-Day Jitters' Ask: *Which word is the adverb?* (totally) *Does it strengthen or weaken 'embarrassed'?* (it intensifies or strengthens it.)

- Display this list of adverbs for the children to sort and write in two groups, 1) modifiers and 2) intensifiers: 'rather', 'narrowly', 'very', 'immensely', 'fairly', 'somewhat', 'incredibly', 'utterly', 'moderately', 'nearly', 'highly', 'extremely', 'partially', 'almost', 'deeply'.

- Ask them to use some of the words in written sentences about the events in Part One. Invite pairs to read their answers to each other. Ask: *Has your partner strengthened or weakened events? Have they understood the story correctly?*

Differentiation
Support: Encourage children to use dictionaries and to work with a partner.

Extension: Ask children to write six to ten sentences about *Wonder*, using adverbs from both groups.

2. Commas, commas

Objective
To use commas to clarify meaning or to avoid ambiguity in writing.

What you need
Copies of *Wonder*, photocopiable page 22, 'Commas, commas'.

What to do

- Recap on the main uses of a comma: <u>a</u>. to separate list items (not usually before 'and'); <u>b</u>. to separate a subordinate clause from the main clause – often using a pair of commas when the clause is embedded; <u>c</u>. after an adverbial phrase, particularly a fronted adverbial. Ask: *What do the uses have in common?* (They make the meaning clearer.)

- Provide the children with copies of *Wonder* and challenge them to locate examples of commas or fronted adverbials and commas for a subordinate clause. (As *Wonder* has American punctuation, it's probably best to avoid searching for punctuated lists as these will contain a comma before 'and'.) Share the examples on the board and ask volunteers to circle the commas.

- Ask children to add the missing commas to these sentences: 'Via who loved her brother deeply just wanted to be the centre of her mother's attention for one night.', 'Jack caught off-guard by Julian failed to defend his friend.', 'Julian brought up to value appearance above everything could not see the wonder in August Pullman.'

- Give out photocopiable page 22 'Commas, commas' for the children to complete.

Differentiation
Support: Direct children to a pre-chosen page, such as the first page of 'Choose Kind'.

Extension: Ask children to write a paragraph about Via, using eight to ten commas to make the meaning clearer.

3. Passive verbs

Objective
To use passive verbs to affect the presentation of information in a sentence.

What you need
Photocopiable page 23 'Passive verbs'.

What to do

- Comment that most of the verbs used by Palacio are active verbs. Remind the children that a verb is active when the subject does the action verb to someone or something else, for example: 'Via *was reading* a long book'. Suggest that the same meaning could be expressed with the passive form of the verb, where the subject has the action done to it. Ask a volunteer to reword the sentence with a passive verb: 'A long book *was being read* by Via'.

- Provide the children with copies of *Wonder* and ask them, in pairs, to find a sentence that starts with an active verb. They then write it on their individual boards and hold it up. Ask everyone to look around the room checking the sentences on the boards are in the active.

- Ask the children, in their pairs, to rewrite their sentence on their whiteboard so that it is in the passive and hold it up.

- Ask the children to complete photocopiable page 23, 'Passive verbs'.

Differentiation

Support: Provide the children with the first one or two words for each of the answers on the photocopiable page.

Extension: Give early finishers a copy of Extract 4 and ask them to identify five passive verbs within the extract.

4. Who, which, where

Objective
To use relative clauses beginning with 'who', 'which', 'where', 'when', 'whose', 'that' or with an implied relative pronoun.

What you need
Copies of *Wonder*, photocopiable page 24 'Who, which, where'.

What to do

- Direct the children to 'The Plague' (the second chapter in Part three) and the words 'which I love to play, too' at the end of the second paragraph. Identify 'which' as a relative pronoun. Ask: *Which noun is being replaced here?* ('Four Square')

- Explain that a relative pronoun and the words following it form a relative clause, an additional part of the sentence. Confirm that 'which I love to play, too' is a relative clause.

- Write 'who', 'which', 'where', 'when', 'whose' and 'that' on the board. Identify them as relative pronouns that may begin a relative clause. Ask the children, in pairs, to locate two relative clauses in Part Three, for example: 'who accidentally touches August' ('Plague'); 'when I got to her party' and 'which is where the party was' ('The Halloween Party'). Read the whole sentence aloud containing 'which was where the party was.' Ask: *What word does 'which' relate and link information to?* ('basement')

- Ask the children to complete photocopiable page 24 'Who, which, where'.

Differentiation

Support: Ask children to concentrate on the first four sentences. Encourage them to discuss their answers with a partner before writing them down.

Extension: Ask these children to revisit a story of their own and add a relative clause to two or three sentences, using a pair of commas as necessary if their new clauses are subordinate.

5. Being formal

Objective
To recognise vocabulary and structures that are appropriate for formal speech and writing.

What you need
Copies of *Wonder*.

What to do

- Recap on the differences between formal (very correct and serious) and informal (relaxed and natural) speech. Point out that the different child narrators of *Wonder* use an informal style. Together, locate instances of August's informal style on the opening page of the novel: contractions ('I'm' instead of 'I am'); casual words and phrases ('sure', 'kid', 'I'm kind of', 'gotten pretty good at'); short, jerky sentences ('I mean, sure, I do ordinary things'.)

- Ask the children, in pairs, to re-read 'Letters, Emails, Facebook, Texts' in Part Four. Ask them to decide which of the communications are formal and which are informal. Afterwards, share words and phrases that helped them to decide.

- Write the following party invitation on the board: 'Master Jack Will requests the attendance of Master August Pullman at the celebration of his birthday on Saturday the twenty-first of October. The event will be held at the Plaza Indoor Centre from two until five in the afternoon. Casual attire is permitted'.

- Ask: *Why is this invitation unsuitable for a child's party?* Ask the children to write the informal invitation that Jack would have sent (as a postcard or as an email) to August, and then ask them to write August's reply.

Differentiation
Support: Organise for the children to role play a phone call about the party between Jack and August's parents before they begin writing.

Extension: Ask children to write a formal letter of complaint to the school governors of Beecher Prep School from Julian's parents.

6. Word relations

Objective
To recognise that words are related by meaning as synonyms and antonyms.

What you need
Copies of *Wonder*, dictionaries and thesauruses.

What to do

- Recap on the terms 'synonym' and 'antonym', using a range of examples, such as 'big' and 'large' or 'big' and 'small'.

- Refer the children to 'The Shift', in Part Eight. Point out the adjectives that August uses to describe the change in attitude towards him: 'big' 'monumental', 'seismic'. Ask: *What is obvious about the adjectives?* (They are synonyms.) *What is the effect?* (emphasis, build up of language, stops repetition and so on)

- Re-read the first page of the novel, discussing the use of the repeated word 'ordinary'. Challenge the children to find a synonym and antonym for 'ordinary' used on this page. ('normal' and 'extraordinary') Ask the children, in pairs, to search through *Wonder* for another pair of synonyms or antonyms.

- Provide the children with dictionaries and thesauruses. Write the following list of words on the board: 'old', 'entrance', 'ascend', 'interior', 'attack', 'short', 'sad', 'interior', 'expensive', 'plentiful'. Ask the children to copy the list and write one synonym and one antonym for each word.

- Encourage the children to use some of the words they have found to write three sentences: one about August, one about Jack and one about Julian, emphasising descriptions and making comparisons.

Differentiation
Support: Provide children with a range of synonyms and antonyms to match to the list words.

Extension: Provide children with these additional words: 'hide', 'genuine', 'bold', 'absent', 'guilty', 'increase', 'transparent'.

Commas, commas

● Rewrite each sentence to include the clause in brackets. Put the clause between a pair of commas.

1. Julian spoke up confidently. (used to attention)

_____

_____

2. His latest games were very expensive. (brand new on the market)

_____

_____

3. Ms Petosa moved on smoothly. (not easily impressed)

_____

_____

4. She chose Charlotte and Miles. (a kind girl)

_____

_____

5. August finally mumbled his name. (keeping his head down)

_____

_____

6. His voice was very quiet. (never loud in new situations)

_____

_____

● Add the 10 missing commas to this paragraph.

For the rest of the day August survived. However lunch was hard. If people thought of moving to his table they soon changed their minds. August when he thought about it did not blame them. If he was honest he was not a tidy eater. Nevertheless a girl named Summer not even in his homeroom group sat with him. From then on the summer table began.

 **Passive verbs**

● Rewrite the active verb sentences so that they become passive verb sentences.

1. Mom made a brilliant Halloween costume.

A brilliant Halloween costume _____

_____

2. Via took the subway for the first time.

The subway _____

_____

3. August used a blue night-light.

_____

_____

4. August overheard a terrible conversation.

_____

_____

5. The conversation overwhelmed August.

_____

_____

6. August threw his costume on the bedroom floor.

_____

_____

7. Via's drama group performed the play *Our Town*.

_____

_____

8. Mr Tushman called August to his office on the last day of term.

_____

_____

 # Who, which, where

● Complete these sentences by completing the relative clause.

1. August was a boy whose _____

_____

2. August and Mom visited a school which _____

_____

3. August liked the boy who _____

_____

4. Summer and August shared a table when _____

_____

● Complete these sentences by adding a relative clause starting with one of the words in the box.

who	where	whose	which	when	that

1. The best lesson was English _____

_____

2. The funniest teacher was Mr Browne _____

_____

3. August wore his hair in a braid _____

_____

4. Henry struggled with the combination lock _____

_____

5. Miranda was August's sister's friend _____

_____

6. The Fairgrounds was the place _____

_____

PLOT, CHARACTER & SETTING ▶

1. Asking questions

> **Objective**
> To ask questions to improve their understanding of the text.
>
> **What you need**
> Copies of *Wonder*, photocopiable page 29 'Asking questions'.

What to do

- Carry out this activity as an ongoing project as you read the book.

- Explain that RJ Palacio makes us continually wonder what will happen to the characters and this keeps us reading. After reading the first five chapters, ask: *What questions do you have?* Share ideas, for example: *How will Via feel about August starting school? Will August manage to stay at school? What will happen to him?* Explain that many of the questions they have will be answered as the story progresses.

- When you have finished Part One, hand out photocopiable page 29, 'Asking questions'. Suggest that the children work in pairs, scanning and discussing what has happened so far. Ask the children to write their own two questions in the first box (ignoring the other boxes for now).

- As you continue reading the book, revisit the photocopiable sheet to write further questions at the end of Parts Two and Three, and to write down when and how the children found out the answers to their previous questions.

- Finally, ask the children to complete the final section with a question that they may still have at the end of the book.

> **Differentiation**
> **Support:** Accept one question at each stage. Offer guidance with finding answers.
>
> **Extension:** Expect more searching questions.

2. Mind reading

> **Objective**
> To draw and justify inferences.
>
> **What you need**
> Copies of *Wonder*, photocopiable page 30 'Mind reading'.

What to do

- Remind the children that although Via is the narrator in Part Two, she may feel reluctant to express any negative views. Suggest to the children that the reader must use inference to understand Via.

- Direct the children to 'A Tour of the Galaxy'. Together, scan Via's list of tasks that she does unaided and without complaining. Ask: *Why does she list them? Why does she mention her young age when she knew not to complain?* Share ideas, suggesting that Via, in stating the facts, may also want some sympathy.

- Point out Via's comment 'Planets are falling out of alignment' at the end of 'A Tour of the Galaxy'. Ask: *What does this mean? Is August becoming more independent of them all?* Share ideas, reminding the children to justify their ideas with evidence.

- Hand out photocopiable page 30, 'Mind reading'. Ask the children to find the four quotations from Part Two and decide what they think Via's thoughts and feelings are at each point, writing these on the sheet in their own words.

- Afterwards, adopt the role of Via and let the children question you about your feelings.

> **Differentiation**
> **Support:** Let children search the text and share ideas before writing independently.
>
> **Extension:** Expect more perceptive comments and evidence from these children.

3. Word discovery

Objective
To explore the meaning of words in context.

What you need
Copies of *Wonder*, internet access.

Cross-curricular link
Geography

What to do

- Ask the children in pairs to scan 'Why I Didn't Go to School' in Part One and locate the place names in the chapter. Together locate Manhattan and Bridgeport, Connecticut on a map. Ask: *Where do you think the story is set?* (America)

- Ask: *What else tells us that this book is set in America?* (the vocabulary) Ask the children to search 'Christopher's House' in Part One for examples, such as: 'Mom', 'bummed', 'fall'.

- Ask pairs to re-read 'Out with the Old' in Part Two and locate two American school customs. (For example: class president, yearbook committee and, possibly, the debate club.) Ask: *What other school customs do we learn about?* (Halloween parade, graduation for each school year and so on.)

- List these words on the board: 'elective' and 'dorks' (from 'The Performance Space')', 'restroom' and 'subway' (from 'After School), 'jocks' and 'elementary school' (from 'High School') and 'recess' (from 'Lamb to the Slaughter'). Ask children to locate each word and copy down the sentence it comes from, replacing the American word with a British eqivalent.

Differentiation
Support: Shorten the list of words and organise for the children to work in pairs.

Extension: Ask children to list six words that should be replaced for a ten-year-old British reader.

4. Who are they?

Objective
To draw inferences such as inferring characters' feelings, thoughts and motives from their actions, and justify inferences with evidence.

What you need
Copies of *Wonder*, photocopiable page 31 'Understanding characters'.

Cross-curricular link
PSHE

What to do

- Explain to the children that readers learn about the characters in *Wonder* in a number of ways: through their actions, words and thoughts (particularly in their own chapters); their chosen friends; and what others say about them. For example, discuss how Summer is an independent thinker and that we know this because she refuses to join in 'the Plague' game and sits with August at lunch.

- Give out photocopiable page 31 'Understanding characters'. Ask the children to search the text for evidence of August, Summer and Jack's characteristics. Point out that they often reveal more about themselves when they are the narrator. Encourage the children to find three suitable adjectives on the photocopiable page for each of the characters and write them under each character. (Adjectives can be linked to more than one character).

- Ask the children to write a new adjective for each character next to number 4.

- Then invite them to use the adjectives they have chosen to write a sentence about each character on the back of the photocopiable page.

Differentiation
Support: Reduce the number of adjectives to choose from.

Extension: Ask children to use the chosen adjectives in a fuller description of one of the characters.

5. Beautiful people

Objective

To discuss and evaluate how authors use language, considering the impact on the reader.

What you need

Copies of *Wonder*.

What to do

- After finishing the book, put the children into small discussion groups to re-read the two quotations beginning Parts Four and Five. Ask them to discuss: *What are they about? Why are they used? Do they relate to the story?* (As the characters learn, it is what we are like inside matters, not our external features.) Ask the children, in their groups, to sum up their thoughts in two or three sentences on a whiteboard.

- Ask the groups to read and discuss the quotations before Parts Six, Seven and Eight. Ask the children, in their groups, to discuss how these relate to the story, capturing their thoughts in one sentence on their whiteboard.

- Encourage the children to move on to discuss the song lyrics at the beginning of Part Three. Remind them of Summer's attitude to August and her contempt for the names applied to him. Ask the groups to discuss: *How does the poem apply to Summer? How does it apply to this story? Why is it placed here?*

- Ask the children to work individually to either create a mind map, or write a paragraph of text, about the theme of beauty in *Wonder*.

Differentiation

Support: Provide references and quotations to help children create their mind maps

Extension: Ask early finishers to discuss the importance of the song lyrics at the beginning of Part One, writing two sentences to share with the class.

6. Points of view

Objective

To read books that are structured in different ways.

What you need

Copies of *Wonder*.

What to do

- Ask: *How is* Wonder *structured?* Write words and notes on the board as the children answer. (parts, short episodes, incidents, different narrators, first person, building a picture, and so on)

- Agree that the book is divided into different sections, each covering similar events from a different viewpoint. Ask the children to check the name of each part. Ask: *What do you notice? What advantages are there to presenting events through children? Are there disadvantages?* (The reader does not learn what adult characters think.)

- Ask the children to imagine that RJ Palacio had written two parts narrated by adults. Discuss who these narrators might be, for example: Dad, Mr Tushman, Mr Browne, Mrs Garcia. Ask: *Which narrator would be the most interesting?* Discuss the views that might come out in each part, for example: *Did Dad's humour mask his worry about August? Was Mr Tushman watching August's class? Did Mrs Garcia smile at August every day? Did Mr Browne know how interested August was in his classes?*

- Ask the children to choose one of these characters. Encourage them to pair up with a child who has chosen the same character and discuss ideas for a chapter. After discussion, ask the children to write the first page of their character's section.

Differentiation

Support: Share ideas in a group with an adult before asking these children to write.

Extension: Encourage children to think carefully about how their character would write and the language they would use. Get them to think carefully about their character's thoughts and feelings.

7. August changes

Objective
To identify and discuss themes and conventions in and across a wide range of writing.

What you need
Copies of *Wonder*.

What to do

- Ask the children, in groups, to write the word 'August' in the middle of a whiteboard and then to surround his name with adjectives and phrases to describe what August is like before he first starts school and what his life experiences are (for example, sheltered, homeschooled, one friend). Next, on a second white board, ask them to repeat the exercise for August at the end of the school year (many friends, aware of others' feelings, confident). Ask the children to share their whiteboards with the other groups.

- Ask the children to suggest the important events in August's journey, creating a class list on the board: going on the summer retreat, leaving Baboo at home, putting himself to bed, seeing Via's play, cutting his hair shorter, the standing ovation and graduation photographs.

- Ask the children to create a flow chart for August's emotional journey. The first box on the flow chart should describe August at the beginning, and the last box, August at the end. In between, ask the children to use four events from the class list, writing one sentence about each event and why it is important to August's journey.

Differentiation

Support: Provide a template for the flow chart and ask the children to annotate it in pairs.

Extension: Ask the children to write a paragraph about each event.

8. Feeling wonder

Objective
To identify and discuss themes and conventions in and across a wide range of reading.

What you need
Copies of *Wonder*.

What to do

- Complete this activity after finishing the book.

- Put the children into pairs. Ask them to explain the meaning of 'wonder' to their partner.

- Display a definition of the noun 'wonder', for example: 'A feeling of awe, surprise and admiration, or an object that creates these feelings.' Ask: *What is the thing that causes amazement and admiration in this book?* (August)

- Explain that the wonder of August is a strong theme in the book. Point out its use in the lines of the song quoted at the start of the book and in Mom's final words at the end of the book.

- Ask: *What else is a wonder in the story?* Write the children's ideas on the board, for example: it is a wonder that Via is not resentful of August; it is a wonder that Summer sits with August; it is a wonder that August is brave; it is a wonder that August finds friends who see the wonder of him.

- Ask the children to write the word 'wonder' as a large outline on a piece of paper (or provide this). Ask the children to fill the outline with words, phrases and sentences on the theme of wonder in the book.

Differentiation

Support: Encourage partner discussion before children write.

Extension: Ask these children to ensure they include sentences about the book as well as words and phrases.

Asking questions

- As you finish reading each of the parts below, write down two questions that you want to know the answer to. As you keep reading, write down the answers and when you found them.

- Write a final question when you have finished the book.

	At the end of Part One: August	At the end of Part Two: Via	At the end of Part Three: Summer
What are your questions?	1. _____ _____ 2. _____ _____	1. _____ _____ 2. _____ _____	1. _____ _____ 2. _____ _____
When did you find out the answers to these questions?	1. _____ _____ 2. _____ _____	1. _____ _____ 2. _____ _____	1. _____ _____ 2. _____ _____

Final question:

Mind reading

- These quotations are from 'Part Two: Via'. Find each quotation in *Wonder*. Write, as if you are Via, what you think is in Via's mind at each point.

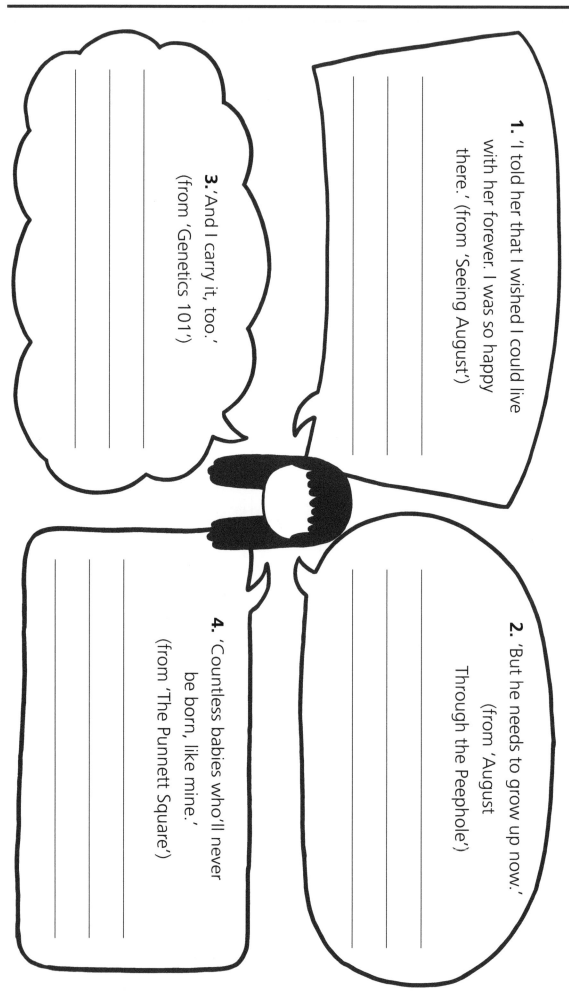

1. 'I told her that I wished I could live with her forever. I was so happy there.' (from 'Seeing August')

2. 'But he needs to grow up now.' (from 'August Through the Peephole')

3. 'And I carry it, too.' (from 'Genetics 101')

4. 'Countless babies who'll never be born, like mine.' (from 'The Punnett Square')

Understanding characters

● Choose three adjectives from the boxes at the top to describe each character and write them in the spaces below. Then think of an adjective of your own to describe each character and write it in the final space for each one.

brave	cowardly	clever	mature	independent	strong	funny
foolish	awkward	immature	dependent	confident	sociable
self-conscious	caring	friendly	thoughtful	special	sensible	different

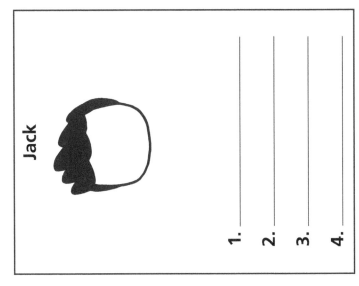

Jack

1. _____
2. _____
3. _____
4. _____

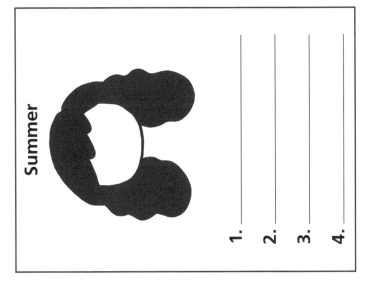

Summer

1. _____
2. _____
3. _____
4. _____

August

1. _____
2. _____
3. _____
4. _____

TALK ABOUT IT ▶

1. Home or school?

Objective
To participate in discussions and debates.

What you need
Copies of *Wonder*, photocopiable page 35 'Home or school?'

What to do

• Complete this activity after reading 'Home' in Part One. Ask: *Why does Mom press her fingers to her forehead and tell August he doesn't have to go to school? Is she confused?*

• Return to 'Christopher's house'. Ask: *What is Mom's attitude to school in this chapter?* (enthusiastic) Contrast her attitude with Dad's. Ask: *What do we learn about Dad's feelings in this chapter?*

• Explain that you are going to have a class debate: homeschooling for August or going to school. Tell the children to pick a side (though encourage them to change sides if necessary.) Ask pairs on the same side of the debate to discuss the statements on photocopiable page 35 'Home or school?' (Point out that some statements may support either case.)

• Ask the children to cut out the statements supporting their case and then write three new supporting arguments on further slips of paper.

• Chair a class debate, listening to arguments from both sides and encouraging everyone to speak. After listening to the opinions, do some children want to change their minds? Have a final vote.

2. Know your mind

Objective
To use spoken language to develop understanding.

What you need
Copies of *Wonder*.

Cross-curricular link
PSHE

What to do

• Complete this activity after reading Part One. Ask: *What do you think about the character Jack Will?* Ask the children to discuss this with a partner, then share their opinions with the class.

• Suggest that Jack is a mixture of strong, good characteristics and weak, bad characteristics. Capture examples of each on the board (he is kind on the tour, he supports August at school, but he is unkind at Halloween, he does not have lunch with August on the first day).

• Point out that Jack could have used his strong, good side to speak up for August at Halloween. Create a conscience alley to give Jack advice just before he answers Julian, with half the class on one side encouraging weak behaviour and the other half encouraging good. Take the part of Jack and walk down the alley listening to the children's advice, for example: 'August is your friend' or 'Surely you want to be with the popular guys?'

• At the end of the alley, reach your decision: to defend August, or to agree with Julian.

• Create new conscience alleys for new individuals to become Jack. Do they reach the same decision?

Differentiation

Support: Provide sample comments for the children and indicate when to speak.

Extension: Ask children to plan a conscience alley for Charlotte in 'Locks'.

3. My Halloween

Objective

To give well-structured narratives for different purposes, including for expressing feelings.

What you need

Copies of *Wonder,* photocopiable page 36 'My Halloween'.

Cross-curricular link

Drama

What to do

- Carry out this activity after reading up to the end of Part Four.

- Ask: *What happens at Halloween?* List the children's points on the board, for example: everyone is excited beforehand, most are disappointed, Mom creates a costume, the terrible conversation in the classroom, Via remembers Grans, Via takes August to the parade.

- Ask: *What does Jack now regret about his Halloween?* (the unkind things he said in front of August) *Did Jack mean them?*

- Suggest that all the characters may want to talk about their experience of Halloween. Tell the children they will be doing this in role, and invite them to decide to be August, Jack, or Via.

- Hand out photocopiable page 36 'My Halloween' and ask the children to complete the cards in character, for example, Via might write 'Think about Grans' and Jack might write 'Look super cool – hang out with August.' Tell the children to cut out the cue cards and use them as they tell their story of Halloween that year.

- After practice, put the children into groups where they can take turns telling their stories.

Differentiation

Support: Suggest working with a partner and keeping the notes short and simple to use.

Extension: Ask children to tell Mom or Summer's Halloween story.

4. Providing answers

Objectives

To take part in role play; to infer characters' feelings, thoughts and motives.

What you need

Copies of *Wonder.*

Cross-curricular link

PSHE

What to do

- Point out that the structure of this book (first-person parts) means that the reader is given direct access to many of the characters' feelings, thoughts and motives. Suggest that it is unfortunate that there is not a part written by Julian, as his actions are an important part of the story.

- Ask: *Do you like Julian? Why? Is his character likely to be all bad?* Share views, suggesting that he probably has some good features. Remind the children that Mr Tushman chooses Julian to take August on a tour of the school and he is very popular.

- Put the children into pairs and ask them to write two different questions they would like to ask Julian. For example: 'Did you feel that you were being rude to August?', 'Was your apology genuine?'

- Create a 'hot-seat' session, taking the part of Julian yourself, and answer the children's questions. Organise the children into groups of four, with one child taking the role of Julian, and the others asking their questions.

- Bring the class together and ask: *What did you learn about Julian? Did you discover any reasons for his bad behaviour?*

Differentiation

Support: Direct children to incidents involving Julian.

Extension: If possible, organise for the children to read 'The Julian Chapter' from *Auggie & Me: Three Wonder Stories* by RJ Palacio (Corgi).

5. Mr Tushman and the school board

Objective

To consider and evaluate different viewpoints, attending to and building on the contributions of others.

What you need

Copies of *Wonder*.

Cross-curricular link

PSHE

What to do

- Write the following headings on the board: '1. Mr Tushman accepts August as a student' '2. Julian makes life difficult for August'; '3. Jack punches Julian'; '4 Mr Tushman allows August to go on the nature retreat'; 5. 'Mr Tushman awards the Henry Ward Beecher medal to August'.

- Ask the children, in pairs, to discuss and make notes about these events. Ask them to discuss: *What did Mr Tushman know? Should he have acted differently?* For example, he has to consider the school's reputation, safety, parents' approval and losing students, his own job security and so on. Remind the children that this is a fee-paying school. Advise them to re-read 'Letters, Emails, Facebook, Texts'.

- Double up the pairs into groups of four. Encourage group members to share their thoughts and to listen and build on one another's viewpoints.

- Tell the groups to improvise a scene in which Mr Tushman is interviewed by the school board about his decisions regarding August and Jack. Ask them to take on the roles of Mr Tushman, Melissa Albans (Julian's mother), and two other members of the board: one supportive of Mr Tushman, the other not.

6. Key moments

Objective

To use spoken language to develop understanding through speculating, hypothesising, imagining and exploring ideas.

What you need

Copies of *Wonder*, photocopiable page 37 'Key moments'.

Cross-curricular link

Drama

What to do

- Re-read the beginning of 'Christopher's House' in Part One. Pause at the point when August hears, for the first time, talk of him going to school. Ask the children to pretend to be August at this moment and to think about how he feels and how he sees his parents react. Ask: *Why is this a significant moment for August?*

- Put the children into groups of four. Give each group a card from photocopiable page 37 'Key moments' and copies of *Wonder*. Ask the children re-read the relevant section in the book, then work together to create a freeze-frame of the moment. Remind the children that every member of the group must contribute to the decision-making. (Ensure that the children who are working on the scene from 'Partners' understand – and are mature enough – to only pretend to punch!)

- Invite each group to present their freeze-frame to the class. Can the class identify the story moment? Ask: *How do the characters look as if they feel?* Invite the characters to say how they feel or let a member of the audience stand next to a frozen character and speak their thoughts.

Differentiation

Support: Move among groups, helping with story interpretation and offering suggestions for poses.

Extension: Ask children to plan alternative freeze-frames, with children changing roles and showing different emotions.

Home or school?

- Do you think August should be taught at home or go to school? Cut out the statements that support your case.

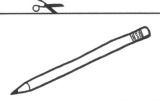

August is quite babyish for his age.

School is the normal learning environment.

August will be able to make new friends.

 There is no one in the school who looks like August.

August is enjoying being taught by his mother.

 August will be taught by more than one teacher.

At home, learning is linked to individual ability.

 For homeschooling, parents can construct their own curriculum.

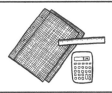 Homeschooling avoids the need for travel.

 # My Halloween

- Choose to take on the character of August, Jack or Via. Answer the questions on the cards from your character's point of view.

- Cut out the cards and use them to tell the story of Halloween.

Introducing yourself

Who are you?

_____

How did you feel about Halloween costumes?

_____

_____

_____

Preparing for Halloween

Were you looking forward to the day?

_____

What did you want to happen?

_____

_____

_____

An important conversation

What was the conversation about?

_____

What was said?

_____

_____

_____

The effect of the conversation

What went wrong?

_____

_____

How did you feel?

_____

_____

_____

Afterwards

How has life changed?

_____

_____

_____

Key moments

● Create freeze frames of these story moments.

Mr Tushman introduces Mom and August to Mrs Garcia. Mrs Garcia has a forced smile and is shaking hands with August. He stares at her glasses which hang around her neck. (Part One: Nice Mrs Garcia)	Jack and Charlotte lead the way out of the performance space. Julian steps in front of August, making him stumble backwards. Julian apologises, but looks insincere. (Part One: The Performance Space)
In Part One, on Halloween, everyone is in costume. Jack tells Julian and Henry that he does not want August as a friend. Unrecognised, August listens in shame and horror. (Part One: The Bleeding Scream)	In Part Three, Summer sits on the edge of the bath, phoning her mother from Savanna's party. Her mother, speaking from her phone at home, agrees to collect Summer now. Savanna is talking to Henry at the party. (Part Three: The Halloween Party)
In Part Four, children are moving about outside the science room to the next lesson. Julian is talking to Jack and he insults August. Jack punches Julian in the mouth. (Part Four: Partners)	Jack and August are returning from the woods on film night. An older boy from another school is shining a flashlight at August's face. A girl looks and screams. (Part Eight: Alien)
It is graduation day. Mr Tushman has just read out 'August Pullman'. August is walking up to the stage to receive his medal as people clap and cheer. (Part Eight: Floating)	Dad takes a graduation photograph of August, Jack and Summer, their arms around one another's shoulders. August is smiling broadly. (Part Eight: Pictures)

GET WRITING ▶

1. 'Locks' précis

Objective
To draft and write by précising longer passages.

What you need
Copies of *Wonder*, computers.

What to do

- Direct the children to 'Locks' in Part One. Point out that it is twice as long as other chapters, and suggest that it could be shorter to keep the story moving. Ask: *Which information is essential?* Let partners, and then the class, draw up a list. (The children are given combination locks; Jack sits next to August; most children do not want to sit near August; Henry creates a barrier with his bag.) Ask: *What is unnecessary detail?* (much of the direct speech; some of the children's names)

- Read aloud the text from 'She picked up the clipboard' to 'when I went up to get my folder'. Recap on the word 'précis': a shorter version of a text. Suggest that Palacio wants to reduce this text of 321 words to no more than 240. Emphasise that important points must be kept with original text as much as possible, but they will want to cut or reword less important elements.

- Ask the children to make notes before typing their first draft précis on a computer. Ask them to then work to get their précis to the correct length. Ensure the children know how to use the word count.

Differentiation
Support: Provide children with a shorter piece of text (already typed into the document) from which they can create their shorter version.

Extension: Give the children a tougher target length.

2. Trick-or-treating

Objective
To select the appropriate form and use other writing as models for their own.

What you need
Copies of *Wonder*.

What to do

- Use this activity after reading Part Two.

- Ask: *Who is the storyteller in Part Two?* (Via) Remind the children that Via is some years older than August. Suggest that this is reflected in Via's writing style. Direct the children to the final paragraph of 'Major Tom'. Point out: mature vocabulary ('dynamics', 'pettiness', 'quivered'); longer, more complex sentences; confident punctuation ('I admit:') and so on.

- Re-read all of 'Trick or Treat'. Identify further aspects of Via's more sophisticated style: realistic dialogue; thoughtful use of paragraphs; powerful verbs ('crumpled', 'bolted', 'sidelined'); effective adverbs ('gently', 'bitterly'); varied sentences; vivid descriptions ('giddy with excitement').

- Comment that Via does not reveal what happens when she and August go out trick-or-treating. Ask the children to plan (sharing ideas with a partner) and write a short chapter in which Via describes her trip out with August. Let pairs discuss Via's likely thoughts: relief that no one is staring; enjoyment of not having her parents fussing over August; sadness that children were mean to him.

Differentiation
Support: Accept less writing, encouraging the children to focus on ideas and structure.

Extension: Expect a longer piece of work with some interesting vocabulary. Expect all elements of Via's writing style, as discussed in the lesson.

3. Charlotte's view

Objective
To note and develop initial ideas.

What you need
Copies of *Wonder*, photocopiable page 41 'Charlotte's view'.

What to do

- Ask: *What do we know about Charlotte? Does she have a major part? When is she involved in the story?* Share the children's answers.

- Ask: *How does she behave on the tour?* (She is polite, she wants everything done properly, she is anxious about Julian's rudeness.) Locate Jack's comment about Charlotte in 'Why I Changed My Mind' in Part Four. ('Goody Two-Shoes') Ask: *What does this imply?* (Charlotte always behaves correctly.)

- Ask a volunteer to read Charlotte's view in the Appendix. Ask: *What does this tell us about Charlotte? Could she have been friendlier? Does Charlotte greet August on the first day of school? Does she sit next to him?*

- Give out photocopiable page 41 'Charlotte's View'. Ask the children to use it to plan out a section of *Wonder* written by Charlotte. Ask them to note down Charlotte's feelings and any useful vocabulary. Ask: *What sort of things will Charlotte be interested in?* (behaving well, following rules, perhaps being nice to the teachers)

- In another session (or two) ask the children to write their section, writing a one-paragraph chapter for each of the boxes on their plan. Remind the children of Charlotte's personality (Goody Two-Shoes) and encourage them to attempt to capture this in her writing.

Differentiation
Support: Ask the children to write a diary entry for Charlotte for the first day of school.

Extension: Encourage children to write perceptively and at greater length.

4. Following precepts

Objective
To identify the audience for and purpose of the writing, selecting the appropriate form and using other similar writing as models for their own.

What you need
Copies of *Wonder*, photocopiable page 42 'Following precepts'.

What to do

- After finishing the book, invite the children to define 'precept' to a partner. Share ideas before referring to Mr Browne's definition in 'Choose Kind' in Part One: 'anything that helps guide us when making decisions about really important things'.

- Investigate Mr Browne's precepts in 'Appendix'. Highlight conciseness; clear, well-expressed messages; emphasis on a moral code. Suggest that by finishing the book with precepts, Palacio emphasises their importance.

- Indicate Henry's precept. Ask: *What has prompted these words? Will the precept help Henry in future decisions?* Let partners collaborate on another appropriate precept for Henry before you share ideas and write one on the board, for example: 'A genuine person provides worthwhile friendship.'

- Direct the children to Jack's precept. Ask: *What could this precept help him avoid?* (serious trouble; struggling in lessons) Work on an additional precept for Jack, for example: 'Always do your best and you will succeed.'

- Give out photocopiable page 42 'Following precepts'. Ask the children to concisely write why each precept is appropriate for that character and to compose a new one. Suggest making rough versions before writing their final, edited precept on the photocopiable sheet.

Differentiation
Support: Provide the children with a list of suitable precepts to match against characters.

Extension: Ask children to write new precepts for Amos and Summer.

GET WRITING

5. You must read this!

Objective
To select appropriate grammar and vocabulary, understanding how such choices can change and affect meaning.

What you need
Copies of *Wonder*.

What to do

- Share reviews for other books the children know. Ask the children to find language use that encourages them to read the book. Point out the features of a review: key information (author and price), who would enjoy it, explanation of the opening set up or hook (without giving too much of the plot away), description of the type of book (funny, scary and so on).

- Explain to the children that you want them to write a review of *Wonder* for a children's magazine. Discuss the vocabulary and tone they will use (probably informal to appeal to a young reader). Discuss phrases and ideas that they will want to use, writing these on the board.

- Ask the children to make preliminary notes before writing a first draft to share with a partner.

- Following advice on how to improve their review, ask the children to write a polished version.

Differentiation

Support: Help children to make notes by suggesting what to include. When writing their review, give them a template to follow.

Extension: Discuss the crossover appeal of *Wonder* and how it has been enjoyed by adults as well as children. Ask children to write their review with an adult audience in mind. Ask them to think what aspects of the book will appeal to adults. Remind them to use a more formal tone.

6. Closure

Objective
To describe settings, characters and atmosphere and integrate dialogue.

What you need
Copies of *Wonder,* photocopiable page 43 'Reaching the end'.

What to do

- As a class, list the essential elements of good endings: tying up loose ends, answering questions raised in the story, resolving plot problems and so on.

- Ask the children to scan through the final chapters. Ask: *Do these chapters form a satisfying ending?*

- Recap on the questions raised in Part One: *Will August cope with school? Will other children accept his physical difference?* Agree that 'Pictures' answers these questions with a firm 'yes'.

- Identify other loose ends that are tied up: August's confidence, Via and Miranda's friendship, Jack's little brother no longer fears August's face and so on.

- Suggest that the big unanswered question is why Julian treats August so badly. Ask: *Should Palacio have answered it in the final chapters? How?* Share ideas.

- Give out photocopiable page 43 'Reaching the end' and ask the children to fill in the boxes with their own ideas for the end of the story.

- Encourage the children to use their notes to plan a new ending for *Wonder* that includes a resolution to the conflict with Julian, along with other ideas of their own.

- Ask the children to write their new ending.

Differentiation

Support: Ask the children to work as a group to fill the plan with ideas. Ask the children to use these to help them write their ending.

Extension: Invite children to plan and talk about a second alternative ending.

Charlotte's view

- Use this chart to make notes for Charlotte's section of *Wonder*. Remember to write as if you are Charlotte.

Opening

(When and where does your section begin? When did you first see August?
What did you think?)

_____

_____

_____

_____

Important events

(Which ones involved August?
Did you see anything disturbing?)

_____

_____

_____

_____

_____

_____

_____

How I behaved

(Do you regret not doing or saying
something? Did you help August?)

_____

_____

_____

_____

_____

_____

_____

Ending

(How did you feel about August by the end of the year?
Do you plan to change when you go back to school in September?)

_____

_____

_____

Following precepts

- Explain why each character has written their precept and write a second for each.

CHARLOTTE CODY'S PRECEPT

'It's not enough to be friendly. You have to be a friend.'

Why has Charlotte used this?

_____

_____

What other precept could guide her?

_____

_____

JULIAN ALBANS' PRECEPT

'Sometimes it's good to start over.'

Why has Julian used this?

_____

_____

_____

What other precept could guide him?

_____

_____

_____

AUGUST PULLMAN'S PRECEPT

'Everyone in the world should get a standing ovation at least once in their life because we all overcometh the world.'

Why has August used this?

_____

_____

What other precept could guide him?

_____

_____

_____

Reaching the end

● Make notes to help you plan a new ending for *Wonder*.

1. Does Julian talk to his parents about his treatment of August?

What reasons does Julian give for his behaviour?

_____

_____

_____

_____

2. Will Julian's parents change their minds about moving schools?

Is there a meeting with Mr Tushman?

_____

_____

_____

_____

3. Does August decide that he should talk to Julian?

What happens to Julian's attitude?

_____

_____

_____

_____

4. Is there still such a happy ending to the story in your version?

Will August win the special medal?

_____

_____

_____

_____

Other ideas I plan to include: _____

_____

_____

_____

ASSESSMENT ▶

1. Making predictions

> **Objective**
> To predict what might happen from details stated and implied.
>
> **What you need**
> Copies of *Wonder*.

What to do

- List the main characters on the board: Mom, Dad, August, Via, Miranda, Jack, Julian, Summer, Amos, Charlotte.

- Comment that Jack, August, Charlotte, Summer and Amos will be in the sixth grade next year. Ask: *How will they behave? Will there be changes in their personalities? How will their friendships change? What details are there by the end of the story and in the postcard precepts to suggest this?* Ask: *What can we predict for the other characters? What might they be hoping for? How might they behave? What will happen to Julian? What does the future hold for Via?*

- Ask the children, in pairs, to choose one of the characters and to write their character's name in the middle of a piece of paper. Above the name, ask them to write words and phrases to capture that character's situation and feelings, along with recent events, at the end of *Wonder*. Next, below the name, ask them to write their predictions, along with an explanation of their supporting evidence, for what will happen to the character in the next year.

- Ask children to work individually to complete the activity for a second character.

> **Differentiation**
> **Support:** Ask the children to focus on August or Julian.
> _____
> **Extension:** Encourage the children to justify their predictions.

2. Grammar search

> **Objective**
> To learn and understand the grammar in English Appendix 2.
>
> **What you need**
> Copies of *Wonder*, copies of Extracts 1 to 4, highlighters.

What to do

- Revise the following grammar points: 1. commas used to mark out a subordinate clause, 2. relative clauses introduced by a relative pronoun, 3. informal vocabulary, 4. formal vocabulary, 5. adverbs, 6. synonyms, 7. passive verbs. List all these headings on the board.

- Hand out a set of the Shared reading extracts to pairs of children. Challenge the children to find one example of each grammar point on the board in the extracts and highlight it. See which pair can complete the task first.

- Compare the examples the children have found. Discuss why passive verbs and formal language were found more commonly in Extract 4.

- Ask children to locate another two examples of each of the grammar points in the novel. Recommend that they start their search in: 'Why I Didn't Go to School' (Part One), 'An Apparition at the Door' (Part Two), 'The Plague' (Part Three) and 'Letters, Emails, Facebook, Texts' (Part Four). Ask them to write out each sentence they have found, highlighting and labelling the grammar point.

> **Differentiation**
> **Support:** Focus these children on locating examples of just two grammar points that you want them to practise.
> _____
> **Extension:** Ask children to compare the vocabulary, grammar and punctuation of August, Via and Summer.

3. Choosing kindness

Objective
To identify and discuss themes and conventions across a wide range of writing.

What you need
Copies of *Wonder,* photocopiable page 47 'Choosing kindness'.

What to do

- Write the word 'kindness' on the board. Ask the children to work with a partner to define 'kindness'. Share definitions, agreeing that kindness involves thinking of others' happiness.

- Suggest that kindness is a major theme in *Wonder.* Ask: *When is it mentioned?* Point out Mr Browne's September precept. Ask: *What is Mr Browne encouraging?* (be kind, in preference to being right) Refer to Mr Tushman's speech in 'A Simple Thing' (Part Eight) and the quotation from JM Barrie: 'Be a little kinder than is necessary'. Ask: *What is meant by this?* Share views before continuing to read aloud Mr Tushman's speech as far as 'An act of friendship. A passing smile.'

- Share examples of acts of kindness shown to August throughout the story: Charlotte says 'Hey' and waves; Summer chooses his lunch table; Miranda includes him in conversations and so on.

- Give out photocopiable page 47 'Choosing kindness' for the children to complete independently. Tell the children to first locate the event in *Wonder,* describe the kind act, then explain the impact on August of this act.

Differentiation
Support: Identify relevant pages in the book and encourage partner discussion before children complete the photocopiable sheet independently.

Extension: Ask children to identify more occasions where characters choose kindness and what they gain by being kind (friendship, perhaps).

4. Being Mom

Objective
To select appropriate grammar and vocabulary, understanding how such choices can change and enhance meaning.

What you need
Copies of *Wonder.*

What to do

- After finishing the book, express regret that there is no part narrated by Mom. Ask: *How would it differ from other parts? What would be interesting?* Explain that Mom would have a different viewpoint and would express herself in an adult 'voice', with complete sentences and more formal vocabulary.

- Re-read 'Costumes' (Part One). Comment on August's simple style: incomplete sentences ('To the playground.'), repetitive vocabulary ('I think'), informal language ('stuff', 'cool') and so on.

- Ask the children to make brief notes on the events of this chapter. After discussion, write chronological notes on the board. Together, consider the events from Mom's point of view. Ask: *Do you think Mom liked August wearing a helmet? Does she really enjoy making costumes? Does she want Dad to take August to school on Halloween? Is she worried about Via?*

- Ask the children to rewrite the chapter from Mom's point of view and in a more formal style, for example: 'I love to see August having more self-confidence. Halloween gives him that opportunity'. Encourage the children to use the notes on the board and to leave the novel closed as much as possible as they write, only opening it to check facts and names.

Differentiation
Support: Provide children with a writing frame with paragraph openers.

Extension: Encourage children to be perceptive in their writing and be aware of Mom's changing emotions.

5. Graduation day

Objective
To identify the audience for and purpose of the writing, selecting the appropriate form and using other similar writing as models for their own.

What you need
Copies of *Wonder*.

Cross-curricular link
PSHE

What to do
- Set the scenario: a year has passed and Mr Tushman has another speech to make. He does not want to repeat himself! Last year he focused on kindness; this year he wants to use a different quality.

- Work together to create a list of other admirable characteristics that Mr Tushman could use for the focus of his speech, for example: friendship, bravery, being yourself, second chances, accepting differences, working hard and so on.

- Ask the children to choose one of these qualities and write Mr Tushman's new speech. Re-read Mr Tushman's speech from 'A Simple Thing'. Discuss examples of formal language, explaining to the children that they will want to mimic this as they write, but they should also remember that Mr Tushman will be talking to children.

- Encourage the children to use Mr Tushman's original speech as a model for their own, particularly the paragraphs beginning: 'We are all gathered …', 'But the best way…' and '…but I want you, my students…'

- Tell the children to write a rough draft to proofread and edit before writing their final version.

Differentiation
Support: Provide some sentence openers. Encourage children to read their draft to a partner.

6. Have I changed?

Objective
To identify the audience for and purpose of the writing, selecting the appropriate form and using other similar writing as models for their own.

What you need
Copies of *Wonder*.

What to do
- Ask different volunteers to read aloud Mr Browne's precepts at the end of the book. Afterwards, focus on December, January and April and ask the children, in pairs, to create more child-friendly versions of these. Share ideas and work on final versions together, for example: 'Have courage' (December), 'Think of others' (January) and 'Appearances do not count' or 'It is what you are like inside that is important' (April).

- Ask: *Has August followed these three precepts during his year at school?* Point out he has been brave by going to school and camp; he is now more aware of Mom's feelings and Via's sacrifices; he realises that people do not keep staring when they get to know him and there is no need to hide himself.

- Ask the children to become August and write a journal entry written by him at the end of the year, in which he reflects on his first year at school. Tell the children to use the three precepts discussed to create a structure for their writing, using each one as a focus for a paragraph.

Differentiation
Support: Provide the children with paragraph openers and expect less writing.

Extension: Ask the children to choose another of Mr Browne's precepts and add a fourth paragraph to their journal entry.

Choosing kindness

- Look up these events in *Wonder*. Who is kind to August? How does this help him?
- Complete each section of the table below.

Situation	Act of kindness	How the act of kindness helps August
On the first day of term, August sits alone as classroom seats start to fill up.		
On Halloween evening, Via goes to August's room.		
In the woods with Henry, Amos and Jack, August realises that he has lost his hearing aids.		

SCHOLASTIC
READ & RESPOND

Available in this series:

Key Stage 1

978-1407-18254-4

978-1407-16053-5

978-1407-14220-3

978-1407-15875-4

978-1407-16058-0

978-1407-14228-9

978-1407-14224-1

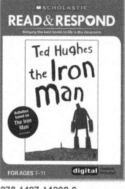

978-1407-14229-6

978-14071-6057-3

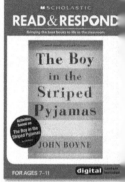

978-14071-6071-9

Key Stage 2

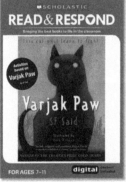

978-14071-6069-6

978-14071-6067-2

978-14071-4231-9

978-14071-4223-4

978-14071-6060-3

978-14071-5876-1

978-14071-6068-9

978-14071-6063-4

978-1407-18253-7

978-1407-18252-0

To find out more, call 0845 6039091
or visit our website www.scholastic.co.uk/readandrespond